6.00

TURNS

by John Matthias

Bucyrus (1970)
23 Modern British Poets (ed., 1971)

TURNS

John Matthias

THE SWALLOW PRESS INC.
CHICAGO

Published by
The Swallow Press Incorporated
1139 South Wabash Avenue
Chicago, Illinois 60605

First Printing 1976

Library of Congress Catalog Card Number: 75-535
ISBN 0-8040-0689-X

Acknowledgements:

Most of the poems in this collection have been published
previously. Grateful acknowledgement is made to *Poetry* for
"Epilogue From A New Home: For Toby Barkan", "For
John, After His Visit: Suffolk, Fall", and for "Clarifications
for Robert Jacoby" (© 1974, 1975 The Modern Poetry
Association); to *The Poetry Review* for "East Anglian Poem"
and "Variations on a Theme by Horace"; to *Encounter* for
"Spokesman to Bailiff, 1349: Plague" and to *Encounter* and
Poetry Nation for "A Painter"; to the *Times Literary Supplement*
for "Alexander Kerensky at Stanford"; to *The Nation* for
"Halfdream After Mandelstam: Who Spoke of the Language
Itself"; to *Solstice* for "Intonations"; to *Beanfeast II* for
"Fathers"; to *Second Aeon* for "May 4, 1970"; to *Chicago Express*
(Special Poetry Issue of *The Third Rail*) for "If Not a Tech-
nical Song American: Statement, Harangue and Narrative";
to *The Antioch Review* for "The Noble Art of Fence"; to *Tri-
Quarterly* for "Three Love Songs for U.P.I."; to *Partisan Review*
for "Free Translation and Recombination: Fragments from
Octavio Paz", "Uncle", "Part Of An Answer", and "Fathers";
to The Wine Press Pamphlet Series for "Double Derivation,
Association, and Cliché: From The Great Tournament Roll
of Westminster"; to *Poetry Nation* for "Three Around A
Revolution", "Born 1851, Henry Demuth", "Bakunin in Italy",
"Zurich to London, Tzara to Trotsky" where they appeared,
together with "A Painter", under the title "Seven Around A
Revolution"; to *Juggler* for "Turns: Toward a Provisional
Aesthetic and a Discipline".

For Diana

Look at these words.
What is there in them
You should tolerate
My absences, my silence.

As if they made a world
Where we could live, you
Offer me what I expect.

Should least. Last. And
Only look on circumspect.

Contents

I

Tunes
   (For John Garvick)

(i)

First time I saw
   him, Segovia,
he wouldn't play.

Now he probably
   can't.

In from the wings,
   holding the
thing like a chalice,

as if it might spill,
   the music, out,
before he played—

you weren't supposed
   to breathe.

Maybe he only noticed
   somebody blink.

(ii)

And only a week or so
   later: E. Power
Biggs at a party . . .

"E. Power Biggs . . . that's
a remarkable name."

Small bones in his fingers
nobody touched.

He offered you his wrist.

Intonations
        (For D.C.J.M.)

Strange that I
should say
it your way
"*Are* you asleep"
to her
and after all
this time
and after all

Are you asleep?
(a stupid question)
No she says
I'm not
and then she
turns and yawns
and then
she is

Are you asleep?
I wonder where . . .
I wonder why
your voice is
in my mouth

Or Into The Bargain

Stranger, agent, sinister
shade, friend of my oldest
enemy's friends

Why do you follow me now
to the railway stations
and airports?

Why is it always
you in the taxi,
gondola, rickshaw?

Open, kindly, to
somebody else's
terrified eyes

Your travel
brochures

Fathers

I never knew them.
Neither one. That
ancient Englishman
was deaf and in-
accessible—I

took his daughter
from his house.
He was dreaming
of ships, of Vienna,
his German assassin

sleeping under
his bed:
I never knew.
In Republican
Ohio, the man

I thought I
hated grew so
thin he'd slip
he said a wedding
ring around his

upper arm. Rheumatic,
he rode like a horse
his electrical in-
valid chair.
He was a judge

and should have
been a sailor . . .
Who'd stand no
nonsense, tell
them of the Empire

and by God Britannia,
chew his pipe
and try to
understand his girl—
twenty-one and

born when
he was fifty.
And if I'd known them,
either one, if I'm a
sailor now and should

have been a judge,
what son will talk
to me? What stranger
take my daughter from
a daughter's house?

Uncle

You were our antique toy
From the twenties, a wealthy
Visitor from Dayton who
Arrived on Saturdays and

Passed out dollar bills.
Your nephews liked you drunk.
"A way of life" you told us—
And sang, basso profundo,

All your fraternity songs.
Before you made your million
You sold balloons to kids
And waited for the war you

Didn't fight to lift you,
Pickled, out of the depression.
And now you have a day nurse
And a night nurse.

When my father died, the best
You managed was: "They had
To stick his pecker in
The pot for months."

And my father in a book he gave
His sister once (your wife):
"For Betty: who doesn't need
A gyroscope to keep her steady."

Survivors

I

A letter arrives in answer
To mine—but six years late . . .
"John," it says,
            "Dear John . . ." and
"I remember absolutely nothing.
What you say is probably
All true; for me those
Years are blank. I believe
You when you say you knew
Me then, that we were friends,
And yet I don't remember you
At all, or all those others
Who had names, or anyone. You see,

The fittest don't survive—
It's the survivors."

II

Like old women, burying their
Husbands, burying their sons, lasting
It out for years without their breasts
Or wombs, with ancient eyes,
Arthritic hands, and memories like
Gorgeous ships they launch
Despairingly to bring back all
Their dead, and which, as if constructed
By some clumsy sonneteer, betray them
Instantly and sink without a trace.

III

Or women not so old—
                           but always
Women, not the men who knock
Their brains and bodies against
Fatal obstacles & spit their blood
On pillows & their hearts on sleeves
At forty-five to die of being fit.

I've known a woman keep her watch
Beside a bed of botched ambition
Where her man lay down & took
Five years to die . . .

And though I drove one January night
Through freezing rain into Ohio—
And though I hurried,
Seeking the words of the dying—
All I found was a turning circle of women,
All I heard was the lamentation of survivors.

Halfdream In Sickness

The bombs my father planted
Go off in my bones; I am weak;

I am sick. Bombs go off in
My chest, off in my back: he

Planted them there, bombs go
Off in my bowels. He stands &

Laughs at me in the past, in
The future: I am the present &

I am completely undone by his plans.
Women gather around: my mother,

My wife. Nothing to do. Lovely
The women who gather around: my

Daughters, but nothing to do.
Love is too hard & I am magnesium

Burning. I am the fuse & the fire.
I am the bombs that explode in my bones.

Part Of An Answer

The man who forced the
window with a wrench
was never there, I
opened it myself: you
suffered anyway your

mugging and his lust.
If we really pulled
our knives in bed
and slashed, you'd
never ask. I'd never

say: responsibility
ends. Your piety!
I'll live on water
and dried peas.
Poems, love, poems!

I try to make the
evil things, secondary
worlds, though even
a Magus said it—primary
there—no world

but the world. And
the Word? A girl
who died for poetry
once wrote: to crawl
between the lines

of print and sleep. She
wanted that. Accretion
then, and possibility.
You wind your watch
and I attend.

Reply To A Valentine

I will hope you accept
My apologies. The delay.
The decay. Dangers may be
Overstressed initially

Or not. But I welcome
This interest of yours.
And I hymn: atlases &
Herbals, occult power.

I have it all in a book
Bound in iron. Can it be
Computed can it quantify?
Quanta is it computation?

You ask. Me! Value error, see?
Incorrect command. Government
Departments are involved with
Overlapping annual leaves.

Should you forget yourself &
With yourself your station,
Enter here litigious & ecstatic.
Your penetrating questions.

Citizens such as yourself.

Atlases & herbals.

Occult power.

If Not a Technical Song American: Statement, Harangue, and Narrative

One: Statement

Just last night I read your poems to the President.
You don't believe me, but I really did.
He broke down completely and
Wept all over his desk.
Now that I've done my work, you can relax.
Everything's going to be o.k.

And I read your poems to a joint session of Congress.
I read your poems to the F.B.I. and the C.I.A.
Now that I've done my work, you can relax.
Everything's going to be o.k.

Two: Harangue

Your tired evasions, euphemism-lies.
Civilized man and his word-hoard.
Will you be relinquant
Or relinquished.

Name and Title. Religion and Rank.
Put a check in the column.
Put a check in the bank.

If you'd be only a little bit clever.
If you'd be occasionally.
If you'd be forever.

If you'd be my government.
If you'd be my gal.
If you'd be my treason and my tongue.

If anything articulate remains,
Identify the numbers by the names.

Three: Narrative

Cachectic, cachectic.
Heart rate grossly irregular.
Jugular venous distention.
Systolic expansile pulse.

Right ventricular lift.
Left ventricular tap.
Murmur along the sternal borders.
Pulmonary edema.

All piezometers installed
In the boreholes.
Static and dynamic
Cone penetration made.

Infra red results
Allow mathematical models.
I hope I was never
Complacent: Seismology.

BUT IF I WAS IN LOVE WITH YOU?
I was in love with you, I think.
I think I didn't have the heart.

No, I never even thought to move the earth.

May 4, 1970
(i.m. Jeffrey Miller, Sandra Lee Scheuer, Allison Krause, Bill Schroeder)

(i)

May 4th and coming from
Chicago thinking '68 and
'68 afraid of getting shot and

now they have for saying things
got shot or their assembly or

because of other people's
notion of decorum

(ii)

Passing the commuter stops,
Hyde Park, gray & weathered
houses by the block-house

high school walls: blackened
letters eight feet high among some

     lesser signals: suicide

and all these voices saying, o.k. o.k.

     they got what they deserved
     they got it like they ought

(iii)

In the photograph you see the situation:
Over someone's shoulder in the picture
In the paper: glance to the side and

     they'll blow out your brains

your cowboy fantasies: your justice that
would stare them down: and there they are, the law,
and plug your people dead:

dead as door mice, dead as door mats
dead in spite of what they said or

what they only thought or guessed
their silliness and smiles:

The other guys are faster and they draw.

Halfdream After Mandelstam: Who Spoke of
The Language Itself
(For Rory Holscher & John Hessler, poets)

I see America closing in on my friends.
Once I was angry; once I protested in poems.
Mandelstam: May 13, 1934: I see
The Kremlin's mountaineer in America.

Words, words: the poem an execution.
They are gunning for Rory and John.
I can see them come in the night.

There is no place to hide.
Their aim is single and passionate.
I see America closing in on my friends.

But I harbor them in my house
With my wife and my beautiful daughters.
There is a knock at the door,
The face of a goon at the window.

They will murder us, simply.
They have been elected to do it.
There is no motivation at all.
Our documents are simple and in order.

Three Love Songs for U.P.I.
(i.m. Karl Kraus)

I-The Army Told Congressmen

The army told congressmen yesterday it has enough of a single nerve gas in its chemical biological warfare arsenal to kill the world's population many times over. But Russia, one lawmaker reported, may harbor an even more lethal capability in this little discussed and highly secret field. The substance is labeled by the army "G.B." and the world's population is estimated at around 3·4 billion. Rep. Robert L. F. Sikes, D-Fla, said he thinks the U.S. is not doing enough in the field. Sikes said it is estimated the Russians have "seven to eight times" the capability of the United States. The U.S. has enough "G.B." to kill the world's estimated population about 30 times. Russia, on the other hand, has enough to kill the world's estimated population, say, 160 to 190 times.

II-A Hippie Type Amateur

A hippie type amateur taxidermist was ordered held without bail on murder charges yesterday in the mutilation deaths of two of four women whose bodies were found in shallow graves in this Cape Cod community. The hearts were missing from the dismembered bodies. Even as police searched by scrub pine studded sandy wasteland for any more bodies, Antone Costa, 24, a currently unemployed sometimes carpenter with a literary fondness for existentialist authors, was arraigned in nearby Provincetown, a summer artists' mecca and hippie hangout. After his court appearance which attracted an overflow crowd including a number of hippies, Costa was committed to Bridgewater State Hospital for 35 days of observation. A plea of innocent to two murder counts was entered on his behalf. Costa, short and slight, with mustache, sideburns and semi-mod hair style wearing "granny" glasses, was taken to the courthouse after Dist. Atty. Edmund S. Dinis disclosed grisly details in the case. About the hearts we'll say: *I ate them for my dinner.*

III-Nomadic Tribesmen Claimed Today Under Oath

Nomadic tribesmen claimed today under oath that the largest known most savory dish is stuffed roast camel, frequently served at Bedouin weddings. Hard-boiled eggs are stuffed into chickens stuffed in a sheep to be finally stuffed up the ass of a disembowelled camel. Rep. Robert L. F. Sikes, D-Fla, said he thinks the U.S. is not doing enough in this little discussed and highly secret field. Sikes said the Nomads have "seven to eight times" our number of Bedouin chefs. Bedouin chefs estimate the world's population at around 3·4 billion. Were there anywhere near that number of camels they might, according to Nomads, serve at their weddings the stuffed roast hearts of District Attorneys.

For John, After His Visit: Suffolk, Fall

Soldati's band shook Patty Fenelon's house
    last Spring so badly that the
Bookcase toppled down and spilled the cheap
    red wine on three authentic South
Bend, Indiana drunks. . . .
                     For you, who love
    the elegiac and, if you believed
The arts you practice had in fact a chance
    of life at all, would prophesy
A new Romantic muse for all of us, how
    can I speak generously enough
About the life we've shared—the rich neurotic
    squalor of the midwest's Catholic
Mecca (. . . you a convert, me a Roman guest—
    cloistered there together preaching
Culture to the grandsons of Italian immigrants,
    the sons of Irishmen and Poles)?

You must, you always told me,
    have intensity. Half your students
Always thought you mad. Like Gordon
    Liddy on a job you'd go
To them bewigged and bearded bearing with
    you some incongruous foreign
Object—a Henry James harpoon or a Melvilleian
    top hat—while through the hidden
Speakers blared your tape of Colin Davis and
    the L.S.O. crooning Elgar on the
Last night of the Proms. Light in darkness, John!
    And all your manic gestures were serene.

Yeats to Lady Gregory, Nineteen Hundred & Four:
    "I did not succeed at Notre Dame."
He began to think his notions seemed "the thunder
    of a battle in some other star"; the thought
Confused him and he lectured badly; later he
    told tales with the "merry priests".
So you were not the first to feel estranged! And
    oh the thunder of your battle in that
Other star, its foolishness and grace. Beyond that
    fiddle, though, intensity was real
Enough for both of us.

How was I to know, returning from the dusty
    attic room where I had gone, where
I had often gone from midnight until three, and
    seeing you stare vacantly across
Your desk and through your lighted study
    window at the February snow that
You should truly be in love with my young
    friend, with that same lonely girl?

Was that the week you thought your son was ill?
    When you waited frightened while the
Severed head of Johnny's siamese cat melted grinning
    in its package of dry ice padlocked in
The greyhound baggage room in Indianapolis? The
    tests were negative, the bites
And scratches healed. . . .
                    Hiking on a treadmill
    at the clinic, I tested badly on a
Winter afternoon myself. I traded polysyllables
    with cardiologists who hooked me to their

Apparatus, checked my pressures, watched my blips
    on television screens, and asked me all
The secrets of my heart. . . .

Once we hiked together on the muddy banks of the
    St Joseph, then across a farm. Your
Children ran ahead. They led you, while you
    talked in words they could not hear,
Haranguing me about the words you sometimes spoke
    when you would only speak, to credit
For a moment, because they looked at all around
    them, tree and bush and flower, because
They did not name and did not need to name, the
    eluctable modality of all you saw.

What more homely elegiacs, John, than this:
    reading backwards in a diary from
May—May to January, January twenty-fifth . . . and
    all my pulses skip. My father's gestures
Of exhausted resignation cease; he drops his cup
    of ovaltine and stares into my
Mother's eyes amazed. . . . No dream, even, did he
    send me in my mourning time, no news
At all. . . . As a child I saw irregularities signalled
    in the pulsings of distended veins
Running up his temples and across his wrists:
    more affaires de cœur. . . .

                  You made
Your trip among the dead ten years ago
    but found a Christian God along

The way in Barcelona. Did I take for politics
    your strange Falangist quips
The day we met?

December last, a month before my father's death,
    a quiet Christmas eve with sentimental
And nostalgic talk, some carolling. . . . Suddenly
    the blood. Stalking through a dark
And quiet house with automatic rifle and grenades
    you'd kick a bedroom door to bits and
Blast the sleeping couple in their bed, sprinkling
    holy water everywhere—your own obsessive
Dream. "I must have savagery", a wealthy British
    poet told me, leaving for the States.
I've gone the other way. My next door neighbor
    pounded at my door on Christmas eve; his
Bleeding wounds were real. What was all of England
    to a single one of his desires? When
I needed help you harbored me.

I wonder if our quarrel touches writing desks,
    like Mandelstam's with Pasternak. The
Better man required none, the better poet did.
    Behind each artifact of any worth,
Cocteau insists, there is a house, a lamp, a fire,
    a plate of soup, a rack of pipes,
And wine. The bourgeoisie as bedrock. Mandelstam
    would crouch in corners listening to
The burning in his brain. If you're a Russian
    Jew because I am a wanton I am Catholic.

So what's the Devil's wage? Your riddling military
    metaphors unwind from Clausewitz and you
Will not say; your Faust, de Sade in neat quotations
    will not do. In London monographs on
Mahler are delivered in the morning post intended
    for the eyes of diplomats on holiday in
Devon—the still & deadly music of the I.R.A. One
    by one these books explode. . . . In the hands
Of an unlucky clerk, the lap of an astonished secretary
    dreaming of her lover.

Stranger, then, and brother! John, these last three
    nights I've listened for you here,
Listened for you here where off the North Sea
    early Autumn winds bring down the
Twigs and bang the shutters of this house
    you came to bringing with you
Secrets and your difficult soul. In disintegrating
    space we are an architecture of sounds.
And you are not returning.

II

After Ekelöf
      (For Göran Printz-Pahlson)

I broke off a branch from
A thin, young tree
Leaving an eye-knot, an eye

It watched as I thrashed
A young bride
On a coast way up in the north

I slept for five hundred years

By a great felled tree
I awoke
On a coast way up in the north

I polished a piece of the thick-veined wood
And over an eye-knot
I painted the face of a mother

Homing Poem

One

An acre, a rod,
and eleven
perches of land

The stone walls
The thirteen towers

And all tithes
& corn & hemp & flax

The stone walls
The thirteen towers

Two

An acre, a rod,
and eleven
perches of land

The stone walls
The thirteen towers

And all tithes
& corn & hemp & flax

The stone walls
The thirteen towers

Variations on a Theme by Horace

Hymns

(i)

Ten times
eleven years

(ii)

(the proper
cycle), may

Songs

(i)

Just a week ago,
remember? when you

(ii)

When you just a
week ago, remember?

Games

(i)

If indirection, certainly; if accidental, rule
The important thing of course is mental attitude

LETHAL CAPABILITY IN HIGHLY SECRET FIELDS

(ii)

Built a tragic theory out of physics

Winds

(i)

A hooded Dane of royal blood
in a little boat with his hawk

Washed ashore on a foreign
coast in a storm

(ii)

An afternoon of falconry
or murder in a private wood

A rival's madness
or the martyrdom
of kings

Ends

(i)

He spoke to
her through a
convent grill

She probably
thought
he was god

Void: fraud, duress,
the night he died

(ii)

The former mrs eugenio said
I am very much happier now

If propaganda ends
does art begin?

New York Power Crisis

(i)

Do not use electric lights
Do not use electric chairs

      Demand is over 7,000,000 kilowatts

(ii)

The new conductor broke his long baton
The hopeless tenor coughed up his blood in his beard

Free Translation and Recombination:
Fragments from Octavio Paz
"No ví girar las formas hasta desvanecerse
En claridad inmóvil . . ."

*

By negation is my increase, my wealth.
Lord, Lord of erosions and dispersions,
I come to you in the whirlwind.

Into the oldest tree I drive my nail.

*

In the architecture of silence
Is no debate between the bees
And the statistics.

Nor is there any dialectic among apes.

The wind blows. The rain obliterates
The mason's mark. On every psalm (on every
Mask of lime) a crown of fire appears.

*

To rattle semantic seeds:
To bury the word, the kernel of fire,
In the body of Ceres:

   poem, poem

Spilling the water and wine,
Spilling the fire.

*

Shake the book like a branch,
Detaching a phrase:

Voices and laughter,
Dancing and tambourines.

This is the winter solstice,
Who will awaken the stones?

Shake the book, detaching a word:
Pollywog, poison, periwig . . .

Say it: a penance of words.

*

But the huddled men in the alleys,
The huddled men in the squares & the mosques,
They took my gems and my grave-clothes.

  I was covered with poems.

In the center of incandescence,
In the column of noon,
I was ringed with sand and insomnia.

  I was covered with poems.

*

And the sophistry of clocks.
And the provinces of abstract towns.

Dizzy geometries, vertigoes.

Not to foretell but to tell.
To say it: a paring away.

Nombre Antiguo del Fuego

     in the tunnels of onyx
       the circles of salt,
   chimerical child of
      calculus and of thirst:

From every stone appears a brief black tongue
Naming the scales of the night.

Once For English Music

(i)

This, this is marvellous,
   this is simply too good—
I am their song, Jeremiah!
   Elgar on The Folk.

And I have worked for forty years
   and Providence denies
Me hearing of my work. So I submit:
   God is against it,

Against art. And I have worked
   for forty years and
Providence denies. And Strauss (R.),
   1905: I drink

To the welfare of the first
   English progressive.
And Gerontius: pray for me, my friends,
   who have no strength to pray.

(ii)

And who would not put out—with his mother
Or his Queen—the night light,

Toothbrush, bathrobe and condom,
Run the bath, switch on the stereo,

Plug in the fire, and wait for time
To reverse, wait for a Prince to rise

From the dead & conduct his affairs?
Neither you nor I, neither mine nor yours.

(iii)

There in the James Gunn portrait,
There, almost, in the Beecham life—

Delius who wasn't really English,
Delius who got around:

Dying, did he summon in his cripple's dream
A syphilitic and promiscuous librettist

(In a summer garden, or on hearing the
First cuckoo in Spring)?

He would compose.
He would have his way with words.

(iv)

During the performance
    of an overture, said Shaw,
By one of the minor Bachs,
    I was annoyed

By what I took to be the jingling
    of a bell-wire somewhere.
But it was Dr Parry. Playing the
    cembalo part . . . on a
Decrepit harpsicord.

(v)

Fluctuating sevenths,
    fluctuating thirds.
I'll play it on my flute
    the way it sounds.

In Surrey, in Sussex,
    airs against the harmon-
Izing organist from
    Worthing. . . .

For Why Do The Roses?
    Because we sing enchanted.
Because we chant
    And sing.

Three Around A Revolution

I-A Gift

He is the Tribune of The People,
He is Babeuf. The others speculate,

But he is Babeuf. The others
Speculate and steal. Gracchus

Out of Plutarch, he takes
The crudely fashioned knife

Made by his son from a candlestick
For his (the father's) suicide.

He hones it on his eloquent tongue.
He says, smiling enigmatically:

Here, it is yours. Do what you can.

II-Alternatives

One announces in papers:
Seeking the patronage of the rich

To further my work. For a decade
It will always be noon.

Nobody's wealth intervenes
Between freedom and time.

One in despair discharges a gun:
Nevertheless, he goes on writing

Noblesse oblige with seven balls
Of shot in his brain.

Making accurate measurements,
Another says: Here we may build,

Here we may bathe, here we may breathe.

III-A Letter

There must be horses, there must be women,
There must be lawsuits. There must, moreover

And eventually, be justice. There must be words.
I write down words. Are we lost in our names?

Yesterday I spoke for hours and nobody stirred.
Rapt. They cheered. I am a hero.

I said words like *action, money, love, rights*
And was moved to elegance, alliteration,

Saying, apropos of what I did not know,
Palfrey, palindrome, pailing, palinode, palisade.

Born 1851, Henry Demuth

Neither wife nor daughter, posterity nor poem
The shops of Soho nor the Soho whores

Could feed Prometheus's progeny
The year of this begetting.

Whose mother was called Lenchen,
Whose sister called him Frederick,

Whose father touched the pulses of the poor
And wrote, and wrote, and wrote

Would drive his taxi through the filthy
Town for years while every bell

In London rang out *Manchester* and *More*!

Bakunin in Italy

Wagner's face is still illuminated
Over Dresden in that fire I fed

And in the glow of it I see my sister
Walking through the snow beside Turgenev.

Did I spit my teeth out in the Peter-Paul
Only to release the homicidal genius

Of Nachaev? I should have been a Jesuit,
A Mason. Castrati sing the Internationale

And dance the choreography of Karl Marx.
I should have been a tenor playing

Sophie Hatzfeldt in an *opéra-bouffe*
By Ferdinand Lassalle.

Zurich to London, Tzara to Trotsky

A black horsehair sofa, Lev Davidovich.
A predilection for exaggerated widow's weeds.

An oratorio by Handel, Lev Davidovich.
A gaudy-feathered peacock under glass.

A red plush chair with a gilt frame.
An enormous mahogany wardrobe.

Face of an Odessa jailer cut in crystal.
A Crystal Palace and a Christian Prince.

Nickname, The Pen; weakness, Beauty.
Already you are old. I have just been born.

A Painter

Marc Chagall knew nothing
About dialectics.

Gaily, daily, in Vitebsk,
Cows & horses danced in the air.

Superstructure he hopelessly
Muddled with structure.

Gaily, daily, in Vitebsk,
Cows & horses danced in the air.

After October, Chagall was
Commissar of the arts for a year . . .

But was dismissed: The Man
Leaping Over The City.

Daily, daily, in Vitebsk,
Icons of Lenin & Stalin objectively stare.

Alexander Kerensky at Stanford

He rose one Winter from his books
To sit among the young, unrecognized.

It was 1963. It was 1917.
He sipped his coffee & was quite anonymous.

Students sat around him at their union
Talking politics: Berkeley, Mississippi.

A sun-tanned blonde whose wealthy father
Gave her all his looks and half his money

Whispered to her sun-tanned lover:
"Where *is* Viet Nam?"

He thought no thought of theirs.
In his carrel at the Hoover Institute

He had the urns of all his ancient enemies.
Their dust was splattered on his purple tie.

Six For Michael Anania

I-Trithemius

Orifiel reigned:
  march 15
    the first year of the world.

So, Trithemius, timid and wise.
So, Agrippa. Light!

Paid the debts at Sponheim.
Drove the lazy monks.
God's breath, good books: stone.

Vulgar speak of vulgar things.
So, Agrippa. Light!

Maximilian in my
  cunning circle
    trod.

II-Agrippa von Nettesheim

Nothing less than total reform
Mystical. Of the world.

Margaret of Austria, O Mirific Maid,

August, divine, and very clement chick,
I'm on the dole.

The Nobility of Women Folk—
Exalt I phrases here . . .
Dollars for the scholars, sweetheart; smile.

So that Franciscan calls me heretic.
So Inquisitor Savini burns his share.

Frogs' eyes. Mule piss.
Everyone's Pythagorean here.

III-Paracelsus

All things change save one.
All things one save change.

Re-ligare means unite again.

Areopagite of Athens,
Follow *now*. Where?

The patients of the Galenians died.

And in her hand
   (the Queen's)
      I'll put a rose.
And in his hand
   (the King's)
      I'll put a golden crown.

And in the sea aboard their ship
The King he'll take his Queen.

The patients of the Galenians died.

IV-Nostradamus

The curious words remain. The seer sees.
Single combat on a lawn; the bloody axe.

Out of time, he travels in it still.
Catherine de Medici knows. Henry II is warned.

The act occurs as it is seen the act occurred.

Out of time, he travelled in it still.
Catherine de Medici knew. Henry II was warned.

The curious words remained. The seer saw.
Single combat on a lawn; the bloody axe.

The act occurred as it is seen the act occurs.

V-Rosencreutz to Saint-Germain

We did not mean Brother Martin.
We did not mean 30 Years War.

We did not mean Huguenots
Or St Bartholomew's Eve.

We did not mean property.
We did not mean money.

We did not mean Pope
Or the Place de la Grève.

But no more maneuvers.
All are vowed to death.

Too late. I have done all I can.

VI

Qualities tend
To Perfection.

We may assist.

Double Sonnet on the Absence of Text: "Symphony Matis der Maler", Berlin, 1934:—Metamorphoses

I

The eschatology of Jews and Christian heretics:
Unearthly metal glows. *Schafft er nicht mehr—*
He lies among his tools.
Geh hin und bilde. Geh hin und bilde
Polyptich as polyphony. Medieval modes,
Matis: Gothardt, Neithardt. Grunewald
To historians, *der Maler.*
Father of no child though, Regina; father
Of his altarpiece at Isenheim, father
Of his torments, his tormentors,
Dying in obscurity at Halle building mills.
Geh hin und bilde. For Albricht, Luther
Or for Muntzer? *Geh hin und bilde.*
The pointing finger of an evangelic hand
Outlasts apocalypse.

II

The libretto: that's the crux, the words.
Because of that the senile Strauss would
Play *Gebrauchmusik* for Goebbels who, while
Furtwängler's applauded by the partisans
Of Brecht or Grosz or Benn, sits
On hams beside the corpse of Wagner.
Oh that Hindemith should feel the pull
Of Matis: What's the distance, then, from
Buchenwald to Yale? *Ist, dass du
Schaffst und bildest, genug?*
Abandoned, all the words: for what
They cannot settle will be left alone.
Leaving us just where, Professor?
Contemplating cosmogonic harmonies with Kepler.
In oblivion with courage and acoustics.

III

"Dissemblers With Their Prince"

Foxes and Firebrands!
Son of a heretic king,
His crafty council, his
Insidious design.

The Word itself in
Vulgar tongue disgusts.
Four square to the
Scaffold: Rood & Shrine!

Spokesman to Bailiff, 1349: Plague
(". . . after which the bourgeoisie.")

We leave you payment.
In a cup of vinegar
Beside the well, the
Coins that you require.

Let no one approach us.
Here we make an end
Of ceremony, custom. In
Our wreckage all of

Europe's racked, your
Kindness unrequited in
Its kind. And yet our death's
A birth of avarice and

Powers oblique, unfathomed.
Leave us bread & ointments.
Free from obligations, we
Leave the world to its wealth.

Having heard how great was the fame that Elfrida, daughter of Ordgar, Duke of Devon, had for her beauty . . .

(i)

So I told him—Look,
You count on Ethelwulf.
Look, I said: my
Comely person and my
Exercise of arms.

A fair accession
Of land, he said.
And it content thee.

That's what he said.
And I said—Look,
You count on Ethelwulf.

(ii)

The King himself
Would have her
In his sheets!

Ordgar, senile
And infirm, I
Tricked him easily.

But now? They
Hasten here under
Colour of hunting.

She ornaments herself.

(iii)

And I must pass
Through the
Forest of Werwell.

And at night.
And alone.

To be set upon by
Desperate men.

To name her name.

Turns: Toward a Provisional Aesthetic and a Discipline

(i)

The scolemayster levande was the toun
and sary of hit semed everuch one.
The smal quyt cart that covert was and hors . . .
to ferien his godes. To ferien his godes
quere he was boun.

The onelych thyng of combraunce (combraunce)
was the symphonye
(saf a pakke of bokes)
that he hade boghte the yere
quen he bithoght
that he wolde lerne to play.

But the zele woned (zele woned).
He neuer couthe ani scylle.

(ii)

And so the equivalent
            (the satisfactory text.
squ'elles sont belles
            sont pas fidèles. rough
west-midland, hwilum andgit
of andgiete: the rest is not
            a word for word defense . . .

(iii)

And make him known to 14th-century men
Even when everything favors the living?
Even if we could reverse that here
I know you've read and travelled too.

So Destination or Destiny: *Quere He Was Boun!*
And yet to introduce the antecedent place.
Restrictive clause; sense of the referent noun.
A tilted cart is a cart with an awning.

> Langland has it "keured"
> John of Mandeville "coured"
> Wycliffe "keuered"

> But "covert" in Arimathaea

Personal luggage: not the same as merchandise.
Cursor Mundi's "gudes"; Purity's "godes"

This is personal luggage / destination / travel

> Harp and pipe and symphonye

> (saf a pakke of bokes)

(iv)

Where dwelle ye if it tell to be?

    at the edge
        of the toun?
    at the edge
        of the toun?

Levande was.
He Levande Was The Toun.

Reason the nature of place
Reason he can praise
Reason what the good-doing doctor said

    Rx. : cart   (that covert was & hors)

Dull ache in the hip is probably gout.
Painful nodes of calcium—(neck & in the ears).
Palpitations, flutters. Stones in the gland.

    food to avoid?   drink

        (put him in the cart)

    Rx.: bibliography
    Rx.: map

(v)

The metaphysicality of Hermetic thought—
Let him think o' that! (Problem is he
Still enjoys cunt . . .)

. . . instrument was ay thereafter
Al his own combraunce . . .

Sary of hit semed everuch one.

Torn between disgust & hope
He simply never couthe . . .

antiquorum aegyptiorum
oh, ... imitatus . . .

(vi)

All day long it rains. He travels
All day long. Wiping water from
His eyes: and twenty miles? and
Twenty miles? Fydlers nod & smile.

Cycles pass him. Cars pass him.
Buses full of tourists . . .
Dauncers & Minstrels, Drunkards
And Theeves. Whooremaisters,
Tossepottes; Maskers, Fencers
And Rogues; Cutpurses, Blasphemers
Counterfaite Egyptions . . .

Greek, Arabic, Medieval Latin,
Mis-translated, misconceived.
More than just for his disport

      who loveth daliaunce

who falleth   (o who falleth)

far behinde . . .

(vii)

That supernatural science,
That rare art should seem . . .

     here among
     a randy
     black-billed

     ilk

Les traductions sont comme les femmes. And time to get off of
her toes. Idiomatic: toes. Lorsqu'elles sont belles. I should apologize,
then: to apologize. The schoolmaster was leaving the village, and
everybody seemed sorry. Simple as that. The miller lent him the
cart and horse to carry his goods. Simple as that. And no particular
trouble with the words. Scolemayster: 1225 in the *Life of St Katherine*.
But you change the spelling, see, to conform with the dialect.
Levande was: *The Destruction of Troy*, "all the Troiens lefton".
But use the participial construction. Sary of hit: see the *Lay Folks
Mass Book*. The city of his destination. Twenty miles off. Quite

sufficient size for his effects. The only cumbersome article (save the pack of books) was: count on the medieval mind to be sympathetic. Though I come after hym with hawebake/I speke in prose and lat hym rymes make. My general principles I take from the King (and his Queen). Tha boc wendan on Englisc. Hwilum word be word. Hwilum andgit of andgiete. Swa swa ic hie geliornode. It would be idle and boring to rehearse. Here what is available. Let me simply indicate the manner. Take sulphur from Sol for the fire and with it roast Luna. From which will the word issue forth . . . *If* the given appeared in a verifiable text. *If* the given was truly equivalent.

The usual procedures are the following: (1) To ignore altogether: "make no effort to explain the fundamentals". (2) To drop apologetic footnotes: "I'm sorry, but I simply cannot understand this esoteric sort of thing". (3) To make suggestive remarks while hurrying on to something else: "*If* the given appeared in a verifiable text. *If* the given was truly equivalent". But the schoolmaster was leaving the village, and everybody seemed sorry. *Jude the Obscure*, paragraph one, a neat linguistic exercise. Written by Thomas Hardy in 1895. And such a revelation makes the art available to the vulgar. Who will abuse and discredit? *Keeper of secret wisdom, agent of revelation, vision, and desire*: THIS IS THE QUESTION WE MUST ALWAYS RAISE.

Now some of the obscure, like some of the lucid, do not become proletarianized. Unlike the majority of their kind, they are not cast down from the ruling class to produce a commodity which both enslaves them and enslaves the exploited labourers with whom they are objectively allied. Perhaps they hold teaching jobs in public schools or universities; perhaps they have an inherited income. In any case, some maintain their Hermetic privilege.

They are not obliged to live by their art or to produce for the open market. Such unproletarianized obscure are revolted by the demands of a commercialized market, by the vulgarity of the mass-produced commodity supplied to meet it. And revulsion ultimately tells (1) on their sex life (2) on their health.

While a relationship of cause and effect is established between obscure and lucid organizations emerging from the division of labour and the consequent dialectical evolution of social reality, such becomes, we know, increasingly separated from the actual productive function of society, from sleep. This gives us pause. "The point is that the notion of invariancy inherent by definition to the concept of the series, if applied to all parameters, leads to a uniformity of configurations that eliminates the last traces of unpredictability, of surprise." This gives us pause.

And so the system and its adherents are the villains; license, conspiracy, and nihilism are the virtues of the heroes: or: The system itself becomes a context for heroics; license, conspiracy, and nihilism become the crimes of the villains; acceptance of convention and austere self-discipline become the virtues of the heroes. The schoolmaster is forever an intermediary: the shape of his life is determined by the nature of society: the nature of his art seeks to determine the shape of society by administering to its nature. And intermediacy ultimately tells (1) on his sex life (2) on his health.

But make him known to 14th-century men even when everything favours the living. Reason the nature of place. Reason he can praise. Reason that he travels in a cart. With Cursor Mundi's "gudes"; with Purity's "godes". With Joseph of Arimathaea, turns: to elliptically gloss.

Double Derivation, Association, and Cliché:
from The Great Tournament
Roll of Westminster

(i)

The heralds wear their tabards correctly.
Each, in his left hand, carries a wand.
Before and after the Master of Armour
Enter his men: three of them carry the staves.
The mace bearer wears a yellow robe.
In rigth & goodly devysis of apparyl
The gentlemen ride.
The double-curving trumpets shine.

Who breaks a spear is worth the prize.

(ii)

Or makes a forest in the halls of Blackfriars
at Ludgate whych is garneychyd wyth trees & bowes,
wyth bestes and byrds; wyth a mayden
syttyng by a kastell makyng garlonds there;
wyth men in woodwoos dress,
wyth men of armes. . . .
                    Or Richard Gibson
                         busy
with artificers and labour, portages and ships:
busy with his sums and his accounts:
for what is wrought by carpenters & joyners,
karrovers & smiths . . .
(Who breaks a spear is worth the prize)

Who breaks a schylld on shields
a saylle on sails
a sclev upon his lady's sleeves;
who can do skilfully the spleter werke,
whose spyndylles turn

Power out of parsimony, feasting
Out of famine, revels out of revelation:—
Out of slaughter, ceremony.
When the mist lifts over Bosworth.
When the mist settles on Flodden.

Who breaks a spear is worth the prize.

(iii)

The double-curving trumpets shine:
   & cloth of gold.
The challengers pass. . . .

Well, & the advice of Harry Seven:—
(or the Empress Wu, depending
where you are):
We'll put on elegance later.
We'll put off art.
No life of Harry the Seven
    there in the works of the Bard . . .
(No Li Po on Wu)
An uninteresting man? Parsimonious.

Wolsey travels in style . . .
                    & on the Field of Cloth of Gold
        & in the halls at Ludgate
a little style . . .
Something neo-Burgundian
(Holy, Roman, & bankrupt) illuminating
Burgkmairs in *Der Weisskunig* & *Freydal*.
Rival Maximilian's mummeries, his
dances and his masques, his
armouries & armourers the mark.
Hammermen to King, his prize; King
to hammermen: guard, for love of progeny,
the private parts!
                    (*My* prick's bigger
than *your* prick, or Maxi's prick,
or James')

(iv)
                    & like the Burgkmairs
these illuminations:—
where, o years ago, say twenty-two or
say about five hundred,
cousins in the summertime would
ritualize their rivalries
in sumptuous tableaux.
Someone holds a camera. Snap.
In proper costume, Homo Ludens wears
Imagination on his sleeve.

But chronicle & contour fashion
out of Flodden nothing but the truth.
The deaths, in order & with dignity,
of every child: I remember that.

Who breaks a spear is worth the prize.

(v)

Who breaks a schylld on shields
        a saylle on sails
a sclev upon his lady's sleeves . . .
And in the north, & for the nearer rival.
Who meteth Coronall to Coronall, who beareth
a man down:—down the distance to Westminster,
down the distance in time.

For the pupil of Erasmus,
for the rival of the Eighth,
a suitcase dated Flodden full of relics.
Shipped Air France, they're scattered
at the battle of the Somme.
It intervened, the news:
it intervenes

As, at the Bankside, Henry makes
a masque at Wolsey's house and, certain
cannons being fired, the paper
wherewith one of them is stopped

does light the thatch, where being
thought at first but idle smoke,
it kindles inwardly consuming
in the end
the house
the Globe

        The first & happiest hearers of the town
        among them, one Sir Henry Wotton

Largely Fletcher's work

(vi)

O, largely spleter werke
that certain letters could be sent
unto the high & noble excellent Princess
the Queen of England from her dear & best beloved
Cousin Noble Cueur Loyall with knowledge of
the good and gracious fortune of the birth
of a young prince:
           & to accomplish certain
feats of arms the king (signed Henry R)
does send four knights . . .

     & sends to work his servant Richard Gibson
on the Revels and Accounts
& sends the children in the summertime to play

& sends the rival Scott a fatal surrogate
from Bosworth, makes an end
to *his* magnificence.

Slaughter out of ceremony, famine
out of feasting, out of power
parsimony, out of revels
revelation . . .

>   As an axe in the spine can reveal,
>   as an arrow in the eye.

Who breaks a spear is worth the prize.

(vii)

And what is wrought by carpenters & joyners,
by karrovers & smiths, is worth the prize;
and what is wrought by labour.
For those who play. Of alldyr pooles & paper,
whyght leed and gleew, yern hoopes of sundry
sortes; kord & roopes & naylles:—
All garneychyd at Ludgate. With
trees & bows. All garneychyd with
cloth of Gold.

>   The challengers pass

83

And deck themselves outrageously
in capes & plumes and armour . . .
And out to play: making in the Summertime
a world against all odds, and with
its Winter dangers.

      In a garden, old men play at chess.
      In the Summer. In the Winter, still.

Who will decorate the golden tree,
Employ properly the captive giant
And the dwarf? Who will plead
His rights despite decrepitude . . .?

      I reach for words as in a photograph
      I reach for costumes in a trunk:

An ancient trunk (an ancient book)

      a saylle, a schylld, a sclev

      a yellow robe, a wand—

      pipes & harpes & rebecs,
      lutes & viols for a masque.

Where double-curving trumpets shine
The challengers pass.

Who breaks a spear is worth the prize.

Clarifications for Robert Jacoby: "Double Derivation . . .", part iv, ll. 1–10; part vii, ll. 1–15, 22–28

A moment ago, Robert, I thought I was watching
    a wren, the one which nests
By my window here, fly, dipping & rising,
    across this field in Suffolk
So like the one we used to play in, in Ohio,
    when we were boys. But it was
Really something that you, Dr Jacoby, would
    be able to explain by pointing out
To me in some expensive, ophthalmological text
    the proper Latin words.

It was no wren (still less the mythological bird
    I might have tried to make it)—
But just defective vision: one of those spots
    or floating motes before the eyes
That send one finally to a specialist. Not
    a feathered or a golden bird,
Nothing coming toward me in the early evening
    mist, just a flaw, as they say,
In the eye of the beholder.

Like? in a way?
    the flaw in the printer's eye
(the typesetter's, the proof-
    reader's) that produced and then
Let stand that famous line
    in Thomas Nash's poem about the plague,
"Brightness falls from the air",
    when what he wrote was, thinking
Of old age and death, "Brightness
    falls from the *hair*".

I wonder if you remember all those games
    we used to play: the costumes,
All the sticks & staves, the whole complicated
    paraphernalia accumulated to suggest
Authentic weaponry and precise historical dates,
    not to mention exact geographical places,
All through August and September—the months you
    visited. You wanted then, you said,
To be an actor, and your father—a very practical
    lawyer—said he found that funny, though
I think we both intuited
    that he was secretly alarmed.

With little cause. You were destined—how obvious
    it should have been!—to be professional,
Respectable, and eminent. Still, you put in time
    and played your child's part
With skill and grace.

There is a photograph of us taken, I believe,
    in 1950. Your plumed hat (a little
Tight) sits sprightly on your head, your cape
    (cut from someone's bathrobe) hangs
Absurdly down your back, and in your hand you
    brandish the sword of the patriarch
Himself, grandfather M., Commander in Chief
    of the United Spanish War Vets.
                        My
Plumed hat is slightly better fitting, if less
    elegant, my sword a fencing foil with

A rubber tip, my cape the prize: something from
    the almost legitimate theatre, from
My father's role in a Masonic play where he spoke,
    once each year before initiations
On some secret, adult stage, lines he practised
    in the kitchen all the week before:
Let the jewelled box of records be opened
    and the plans for the wall by the
South west gate be examined!

The photographer, it seems, has irritated us.
    We scowl. The poses are not natural.
Someone has said Simon says stand here, look
    there, dress right, flank left;
Someone, for the record, intervenes. Or has
    James arrived? Our cousin from the
East side of Columbus who, with bicycles
    and paper routes and baseballs
Wanted you in time as badly then as I could
    want you out of it. A miniature
Adult, he looked askance at our elaborate
    rituals. He laughed outright,
Derisively. No mere chronicler, he was reality
    itself. I hated him.

Of whom I would remind myself when asking you:
    do you remember? a world of imagination,
Lovely and legitimate, uncovering, summer after
    summer, a place that we no longer go,
A field we do not enter now, a world one tries
    to speak of, one way or another,

In a poem. Robert! Had the jewelled box
    of records been opened and the plans
For the wall by the south west gate been examined,
    news: that he, not you and I, made
Without our knowledge, without our wigs and
    epaulets, with bricks he had a right
To throw, binding rules for our splendid games.

How remote it all must seem to you who joined
    him with such dispatch. One day, I
Suppose, I'll come to you in California saying
    to you frankly: cure me if you can.
Or to some other practising your arts. Until then,
    what is there to talk about except
This book of photographs? And what they might
    have made of us, all those aunts,
Clucking at our heels, waddling onto Bosworth field
    or Flodden with their cameras. And why
They should have come, so ordinary and so mortal,
    to bring back images like this one
Turning yellow in a yellow book. Brightness fell
    from the hair

Of whom I would be worthy now, of whom I think
    about again as just outside my window
A child plays with a stick. And jumps on both feet
    imitating, since she sees it in the field
(With a stick in its beak), a wren. She enters
    the poem as she enters the field. I will
Not see her again. She goes to her world of stick
    and field and wren; I go to my world

Of poem. She does not know it, and yet she is here:
     here in the poem as surely as there
In the field, in the dull evening light, in the world
     of her imagining, where, as the mist descends,
She is a wren.

As I write that down she is leaving the field.
     She goes to her house where her
Father and mother argue incessantly, where
     her brother is sick. In the house
They are phoning a doctor. In the poem—
     because I say so,
                              because I say once more
That she enters the world of her imagining
     where, as the mist descends,
She is a wren—
     She remains in the field.

The Noble Art of Fence: A Letter

Ardent fight stayeth a gardant fight
   or putteth backe
   or beateth

Open fight stayeth an open fight
Variable answereth variable
Close fight is beaten by gardant fight

Slowfoot: swift hand   Quickfoot: slow hand

   tread, stride, follow, fallaway

. . . they seek a true defense in an untrue sword.
Rapiers! Frogpricking poniards! The strange devices of
Italians and the French. Toys fit to murder poultrie, I
should say. My Lord:

       THEY BRING THEIR LIVES
TO AN END BY ART

     Can they pierce a corslet
       or unlace a helmet strap?
     Can they hew asunder pikes?

     tempestuous terms

       stocata, dritta, reversa

     our best men fall to style.

Speak not evil? Behind the backs of Men? Dispraise no play
nor workmanship? But Italians! We answer the bragging
strangers, we point: Signior Rocko and Signior Rocko
his son

with false play or plaine
with broken shins, cracktpates.

. . . for Rocko came to town, all right, and built
himself a fancy place in Warwicke Lane. Not a fencing-school,
mind you, but a *college*. Styled himself the World's Greatest
Master Of The Art. (And teaching *offense!*) His scholars—
noblemen and gentlemen of the court—would set up their arms:
and under these their gear: rapiers and daggers, gloves of
mail and gauntlets. . . . He was the darling of the sycophants and
courtiers: much beloved by men who never need to draw a sword,
men of elegance and wit, men of leisure, poets: men who can
afford a fashion or a style. One day Austen Bagger, being merrie
and amongst his friends, took his Sword and Buckler and his valiant
heart off to Warwicke Lane, and standing there upon his skill he
shouted: ROCKO, YOU FAGGOT, UP YOUR ASS WITH BOATMEN'S OARS
AND BATTLE AXE AND PIKE. UP YOUR ASS WITH RAPIERS . . .

And down came Rocko with his two hand sword
And manfully did Austen Bagger close with him
And stroke up his heels
And cut him under the breech . . . .

Shall I admonish against quarrels and brawls?
I tell you: Judgment, Distance; Time & Place & Measure
I do not darkly ryddle here
I set it down

I choose, my Lord,
　　　　the short and ancient weapons of our land.

The times are difficult, and have been. I tell you plainly that our
Masters of Defense are thought by those who flatter Bobadill to be so
many vagabonds and bearwards. The city fathers, fearing, as they say,
the plague, will have no prizes played in London. But any haberdasher
sells to any cobbler bucklers. Every serving man will play with hilted
cudgels squawking in the language of Italian schools. But Richard Beste?
Gunner at the Tower. William Hearne? Yeoman of the guard. William
Joyner? Tavern keeper. John Evans? Jerkin-maker. Honest men and masters
of a mystery, but all of them pretending trades because the Law from
Coke and Blackstone on has always here and still will threaten penalties . . .

I mean the Statute of Rogues
I mean the Vagrancy Act
I mean to say I'm not among the lewd and dissolute who'd
　　　　covet singular advantage without license or authority or oath

　　　　　　I'd teach a man to fight!

92

So here's
our bargain Sir
and guild or no incor-
poration patent royal favour
ipso facto lawful sworn I swear it
on a hilt which is to say the cross KNOW
YE THAT WE admit all provosts of sufficient
cunning expert tried before us masters of the science
openly within the city giving scholars first a warning twenty
days and then to playe their prize by god or sovereign lady queen
of england france and ireland all her sherif baylif's deputies and con-
stables we certify commission and we license deputize defenders of the realm

      of england by the grace of god amen

The weapons are not rapiers. The weapons are the longsword sword and
buckler backsword sword and dagger stave or pike the great two-handed
sword the single dagger javelin the partisan the black bill glaive
and half-pike battle axe . . .   and these are times:

           The time of the hand
              The time of the hand and bodie
                  The time of the hand, bodie and foot

           The time of the foot
              The time of the foot and bodie
                  The time of the foot, bodie and hand

. . . this is not mathematics this is movement. This is not manners: This is not ballet. Whatsoever is done with the hand before the foot or feet is true. Whatsoever is done with the foot or feet before the hand is false. I tell you: Judgment, Distance; Time & Place & Measure. I tell you grips and wrestlings. I tell you thrusts and blows. Treading of ground, doubles, wards, closing and breaking, knees to the groin, boot in the ass, knife in the eyes: There *is* no observation of Italian niceties in War.

And now there are more of them.
I mean Saviolo and Co.

Business is bad . . . .

. . . our poets advertise their doings on the stage and yet not one of them will play his prize. They stay indoors and write their books and talk of etiquette. They read Castiglione, draw their diagrams from Euclid, darn their hose, inspire all diversities of lies. All of them are pederasts. They dance the galliard and pavane, they vault most nimbly, oh they caper loftily these warlike souls who translate greek and perish from the French disease . . . .

Hieronimo, go by. Well *he* got *his* at least.

They'll touch the weapons of another man that weareth them yet deal with all punctilio to be observed. They talk of noble ancestors in Rome . .

They boast outrageously
  They dye their beards
 They only feign
  They will not fight

   These euphuistic lurid sodomites . . .

TAKE UP FENCING! Drive away all aches and pains; drive away disease and grief, make a nimble body, get thee strength. It sharpeneth the wit, expelleth choler, melancholy, many other vile conceits: it keepeth man in breath, in perfect health, it makes him to be long of life who useth it . . . Item, item, item! You shall swear so help you god that you shall uphold and maintain such articles as shall be here delivered unto you . . . Item, item, item! Loving truth and hating falsehood you shall be a master to the last day of your life. Item, item, item! You shall not any suspect person teach, no murderer nor common quarreler no drunkard no nor shall you mix with them . . .

You shall be merciful.
You shall love and honor him who taught you cunning.

                    useless!

   item, item, item . . .

I weep for master Turner: murdered with a pistol from behind.
I weep for Henry Aldington: hanged.

95

I weep for Furlong: drunk a pint of aqua vita straight off
    in one go; then he fell down dead.
I weep for Westcott: suicide.

. . . for there are wicked angels which are waiters

and attend upon ungodly life . . . attend upon

                        the time of the hand
                            the time of the hand and bodie
                                the time of the hand, bodie and foot

. . . and then he need not fear to say Come Quickly: today
or tomorrow, or when thou wilt, and with what manner of death soever,
so it come by thine appointment . . .

I think I'll go get Saviolo myself.
I'll challenge him, call him out of his
Elegant house, away from his elegant friends.

I'll close with him. I'll strike up his heels.
I'll cut him under the breech.
I'll take his scalp. I'll take his scalp.

I'll vanish quick (quick!) to Illyria.

East Anglian Poem

I

Materials of Bronze and of Iron—

  linch-pins and chariot wheels, nave-bands
and terret-rings: harness mounts, fittings, and
bridle-bits: also a sword, an axe: also a
golden torc

> But the soils
> are acid here
>
> and it rains

Often there's only the mark of a tool on a bone
Often there's nothing at all

II

They herded oxen and sheep   They hunted the deer
They made a simple pottery, spun yarn   They scratched
in the earth to little effect

> They were afraid

> of him

> here, with his armour

> > thigh and skull unearthed
> > > beside the jawbone of his horse

Afraid of him who
    feared these others, Belgae,
speaking Celtic too, but building oppida, advancing,
turning sod with coulters and with broad-bladed ploughs.

> (Caesar thought them civilized—
> > which meant familiar

> They minted coins

> They made war on a sophisticated scale)

III

Sub Pellibus:

> Rectangular tents in orderly lines
> and round the camp a ditch.
> Palisade stakes. Rows of javelins
> with soft iron shanks, the semi-
> cylindrical shields.

>> Second Augusta here—
> with auxilia: archers and slingers,
>>> mercenary Gauls.

He saw them on parade:

> their elegant horses, their leathers
> studded with gilt, their silvered pendants and
> the black niello inlay of their fittings
> and their rings

> their helmets made an apparition
> of the face: apertures for eyes. Their
> jerkins were embroidered, their yellow plumes and
> scarlet banners sailed in the wind.

> So they'd propitiate their gods.

He saw them on parade:

    to his north and east
the boundary was the sea
    iron pikes were driven
in the Waveney and Yare
    to his west the fenlands
forest to the south
    and south as well
between the trees and fens
    at Wandlebury here
along a narrow belt of chalk
    no more than eight
miles wide

        his ramparts rose

      (where certain grave-goods lie)

IV

Within his hornworks
Behind his stone and timber walls
Below his towers and beneath his ample crop

    these early dead

        (he saw the Trinovantes destroyed
        who later saw Caratacus in chains)

    Their armlets and their
    toe-rings still adorn. Bronze
    bowls, amphorae, still provide.

    . . . and magic tokens there
    and writings there corrupted.
    With all their stolen coins,
    a carnyx there to play.

    And stood up in the marshes many days.
    Nor cried for meat.
    Nor longed for any cup.

Consider what they were before
that men could suffer labor.

And feed upon the roots and barks of trees.

V

Before him and unknown to him and
southward came the stones: dolerite-blue
with tiny bits of felspar. From the Mt. Prescelly
outcrops—Carn Meini, Foel Trigarn

"Lord, and you must climb the holy peak"

Before him and unknown to him
the first charioteers
Before him, the first tamer of horses.

He saw the hare run
toward the sun, the

mistletoe and sickle
in the tree

From the woods and the bogs
they began to assemble

After the flat-bottom boats in the shallows of Mona

VI

After the incantations and the libations
After the auguries in the grove of the dishonored queen
After the spectral bride at the mouth of the Thames

       Did the tethered swans fly above him?
       Did the deer follow behind?

And after the pounding of magic into the swords?

From the confiscated lands
From the Calendar of Rites
From the Forward Policy of Rome

From the open hands of
      frightened and obsequious client-kings
From the pride of the Legatus
From the procurator's greed

       From the Divine House of Tiberius Claudius
         His octastyle temple and His Name
       NUMEN AUGUSTI
         From the hands of the Goddess of Death

The tethered swans flew above him
And the deer followed behind

Epilogue From A New Home:
For Toby Barkan

There's a plague pit
    just to the edge of the village.
Above it, now mostly covered with grass,
    a runway for B-17s: (American
Pilots back from industrial targets). Tribes
    gathered under my window;
They'd sack an imperial town: I'll wave
    to my wife at the end of the Roman road.

At night I said
    (the odd smell of the house recalling home)
"My father sits up in his grave.
    I'm too unstrung to love you now. Look:
Children play in the garden with bones."

Enclosed within a boundary of stones
    they died in isolation. All of us have
Colds; we visit the parish church and read: "Names.
    The numbers of persons who died of bubonic plague."
Grey-stone cottages across the road,
    a stream at the end of the church-yard,
Giant harvesters working the mechanized farms. . . .

Yesterday I walked to see the black,
    malignant huts that held the bombs.
After the war, nobody tore them down. Some
    are full of hay. Mechanics counted, standing
There, the number of planes that returned. I don't
    understand the work men did in the fields, or do.

I don't know the names of the crops. I don't
    know the uses of gears.
A church has grown on every hill like a tree.

Green on green: texture, shade, & shadows:
    opening out, folding in, surrounding.
Before the planes, someone counted ships: counted
    once that ancient one across the Deben
Where, from Woodbridge, you can almost see the site
    where his retainers set about to bury it,
A cenotaph, a King's.

Cynouai says: "I don't like my name. I won't have
    a name and I'll just be a girl."
Laura, three and deferential, understands. I open
    a bottle of wine.

A whir of looms where wool was wealth:
    (*nidings voerk*, *nidings voerk*) the baths long
Drained, the polyglot army long before withdrawn.
    If the Trinovantian coins & the legionary oaths,
If the pentatonic lyre in the Royal Ship
    prefigure here a merchant—*upon his head
A Flaundrish bever hat—*,
                          is that more odd
    than that my children's rhyme recalls
The plague, the unattended fields & the dissipation
    of the feudal claims, or that the final
Metamorphosis of Anna's luck should find its
    imagery—like Christ's—in bas-reliefs
Depicting animals domesticated by domesticating
    Saxon heirs?

We picnic by these graves, these strata of
     the dead: Celtic, Roman, Viking, English—
All of them killers, all of them dead, they'd moralize
     on one another's end. Christian to pagan, power
To power, and I am also implicated here: the woodwose
     in the spandrels of a door lifts up his club,
A voice begins to speak of Fifteen Signs. . . .

Ah, Toby Barkan,
     this is not the poem you asked me for.
Waiting for the Wickham Market train a year ago I
     sat near Liverpool Street and wrote down notes:
About your early marriage and the joy of it,
     about the way it lasted—all that joy:
About a painting left unfinished for a year,
     a painter saying that he wanted more
From life than art—
     more than just to be competent:
Meaning that he wanted you instead,
     and his son, my oldest friend,
And his son's wife,
     and his son's son and his daughter . . .

And meaning, I suppose,
     that competence is dangerous and deceptive,
Meaning that he'd quit:
     before he tricked himself, before he'd
Grown so old he'd suffer for it all.

And I wrote down notes about his
    playfulness, his pranks,
His driving you through mud—
    a badly marked provincial road—
Looking for something, he didn't know what,
    and sinking you up to the hubcaps,
And how you saw it then:
    the spring fields, the splendour.

I never wrote that poem.
    I wrote down words—none of them mine—
That ought to count for more:
    the Russian *Zhizneradostny*,
Which isn't "cheerful" or "joyous",
    but even better: "life-glad."
From Brecht I wrote down *Freundlichkeit*,
    from Chaucer: *Gentilesse*.

Ah, Toby, what a thing to ask me.
    To write a poem about your husband,
Dead from cancer, whom I never really knew.
    And you were perfectly serious,
Wondering: couldn't I catch something
    of his life?
You'd tell me stories, give me the details:
    for he was life-glad and gentle,
He was kind . . .

In a hall at Aldeburgh an attentive audience is
    momentarily distracted by the jet (American—
The base hasn't moved very far) which flies above them
    as they listen to a song by Britten
Or by Gustav Holst. Where Thomas Hardy prayed
    (dismaying Clodd, his scientific friend),
Where George Crabbe's father preached,
    is space, is history made soluble in art,
A good man's life made durable? Cynouai is bored,
    Laura is tired. As the plane approaches,
Both of them look up. If they could understand;
    If I could let them know.

Oh, I remember you that day: the terror in
    your face, the irony and love. And I remember
What you wanted me to do. That ancient charge: to
    read whatever evidence in lives or lies appears,
In stones or bells—transform, transfigure then whatever
    comedy, catastrophe or crime, and thus
Return the earth, thus redeem the time. And this:
    to leave it all alone (unspoken always: look, I have
This moment and this place): *Cum on, cum on my owyn
    swet chyld; goo we hom and take owr rest . . .*
Sing we to the oldest harpe, and playe . . . Old friend,
    old debt: I'm welcoming at last your presence now.
I'm but half oriented here. I'm digging down.

Notes

One takes what one needs, but with thanks and praise. I have plundered various sources as indicated below (1) to get my general bearings in the course of a composition or (2) for passages and fragments which provide documentary material in which poetic energy can be isolated so as to expand the voicing of particular parts of this book—sometimes quoting, sometimes translating or transmuting them (vide *Turns*). A poet's often random, pretty unscholarly (though sometimes purposeful) reading over certain periods of time when engaged in assembling certain kinds of structures.

W. H. Auden, *Secondary Worlds*; Robert Duncan, Introduction to *Bending the Bow*; Sylvia Plath, *The Bell Jar*; A. Alvarez, *The Savage God* ("Part of an Answer"). Stéphane Mallarmé, "Prose—pour des Esseintes" ("Reply to a Valentine"). George Steiner, *Extraterritorial*; Osip Mandelstam, the epigram on Stalin ("Halfdream After Mandelstam: Who Spoke of The Language Itself"). United Press International Wire Service ("Three Love Songs for U.P.I."). Nadezhda Mandelstam, *Hope Against Hope*; John Garvick, his great but so far untranscribed oral masterpiece; tags from Yeats, Joyce, de Sade, Octavio Paz, Jean Cocteau ("For John, After His Visit: Suffolk, Fall"). Gunnar Ekelöf, "Xoanon": *Selected Poems* translated by W. H. Auden and Leif Sjöberg with an Introduction by Göran Printz-Pahlson ("After Ekelöf"). Horace, *The Odes* ("Variations on a Theme by Horace"). Octavio Paz, *Configurations* ("Free Translation and Recombination: Fragments from Octavio Paz"). F. S. Howes, *The English Musical Renaissance* ("Once for English Music"). Edmund Wilson, *To The Finland Station* ("Three Around A Revolution", "Born 1851, Henry Demuth", "Bakunin in Italy"). Kurt Seligmann, *A History of Magic* ("Six for Michael Anania"). Paul Hindemith, *Libretto: Matis der Maler*; Otto Benesch, *The Art of the Renaissance In Northern Europe*, Chapter II; Ian Kemp, *Hindemith*; F. W. Sternfeld, ed., *Music in the Modern Age*, Chapter 2: "Germany", Elaine Padmore; Norman Cohn, *The Pursuit of the Millennium* ("Double Sonnet on the Absence of Text: 'Symphony Matis der Maler', Berlin, 1934:—Metamorphoses"). Anon., *A History of Framlingham* ("Dissemblers With Their Prince", "Homing Poem", "Having heard how great was the fame that Elfrida, daughter of Ordgar, Duke of Devon, had for her beauty . . ."). R. B. Dobson, ed., *The Peasants' Revolt of 1381* ("Spokesman to Bailiff, 1349: Plague"). Thomas Hardy, *Jude the Obscure*; H. T. Low Porter, translator's note, *Dr. Faustus*; A. F. E. Burroughs, *West Midland Dialects of the 14th Century*; J. Matthias, *Bucyrus* and *Th' Entencioun and Speche of Philosophres*; tags from King Alfred, Chaucer, Langland, John of Mandeville, Wycliffe, the *Pearl* poet, Joseph of Arimathaea; George Steiner, *Language and Silence* ("Turns"). *The Great Tournament Roll of Westminster, A Collotype Reproduction of the Manuscript*: Sydney Anglo's Historical Introduction, Appendices I and II—Tiptoft's Ordinances and the Revels Account of Richard Gibson, and the Analytical Description; Gordon Donaldson, *Scottish Kings*; Lt. Colonel Howard Green, *Battlefields of Britain and Ireland*; Peter Alexander, Introduction to Shakespeare's (?) *Henry VIII* in the *Collins Tudor Shakespeare* ("Double Derivation, Association, & Cliché: from *The Great Tournament Roll of Westminster*"). Joseph Swetnam, "Epistle to the Reader" & "Preface to Professors" in *The Noble Science of Defence*; George Silver, *The Paradoxes of Defence* and *Brief Instructions Upon My Paradoxes of Defence*; J. D. Aylward, *The English Masters of Arms*; A. L. Soens, "Lawyers, Collusions and Cudgels: Middleton's *Anything For a Quiet Life*, I.i. 220–221", *English Language Notes*, Vol. VII, No. 4 ("The Noble Art of Fence: A Letter"). Tacitus, *The Annals of Imperial Rome*, chapters 10 and 12; Stephen Gosson, *School of Abuse*; R. R. Clarke, *East Anglia*, chapters 6 and 7; I. A. Richmond, *Roman Britain*, chapters 1, 2, and 5; Donald R. Dudley and Graham Webster, *The Rebellion of Boudicca*; Patrick Crampton,

Stonehenge of the Kings, chapter one; Ronald Blythe, ed., *An Alde-burgh Anthology* ("East Anglian Poem" and "Epilogue From a New Home: For Toby Barkan"). Other debts—especially those to poets—are numerous but, I trust, obvious: whether in the charac-teristic adjective or in the full scale rite of homage.